Higher Glyphics

Jack Kolkmeyer
Delray Beach, Florida

First Published in 2016
Published by:
FORTE Publications
#12 Ashmun Street
Snapper Hill
Monrovia, Liberia

FORTE Publishing
7202 Tavenner Lane
208 Alexandria
VA, 22306

FORTE Press
76 Sarasit Road
Ban Pong, 70110
Ratchaburi, Thailand

http://fortepublishing.wix.com/fppp

This book or any portion thereof may not be reproduced or used in any manner whatsoever without the express written permission of the publisher except for the use of brief quotations in a book review.

Printed in the United States of America

Photographer: Jeff Nelson/Santa Fe

Copyright © 2016 JACK KOLKMEYER
All rights reserved.

ISBN-10: 0994534744
ISBN-13: 978-0- 9945347-4- 3

Dedication

Higher Glyphics
is dedicated
to all those who seek the truth
and
to a deeper understanding
of the worlds around us

Special thanks to
Forte Publications
for believing in
these words

Table of Contents

Dedication iii
Table of Contents v
Notes viii
Assembly 1
The Standing Stones 2
Dolmen Time 4
Born Again 6
Scattered Fragments 7
Inching Along..9
Journey to the Center of the Core....................10
Chicken Bone Juju...12
Still Stoned 14
Small is Beautiful...16
People of a Different Mind 19
Let the Tree Fall 20
The Geo Logics of Flood 21
Mending the Fence...23
Sitting in a Long Gone Bar 26
The Heart of Greenness 27
Triple Plays..33
Sun Spurts...35
Take the Fifty Fifty Road 36
This Is Not a Weed..37
In a Vara Way Land 39
Push Has Come to Shove 41
About the Author...42

Notes

Glyphs or glyphics have existed in almost every form of civilization.

The ancient ones and the ancestral voyagers of other times have left so many messages for us around the planet to help us better understand who we are, where we came from and just where we might be headed. Messages written in strange alphabets and with anthropomorphic symbols, but each with a specific point of view.

Higher Glyphics ponders some of these messages.

Cover Photo Credits:

Photographer: Jeff Nelson/Santa Fe

Photo: Sego Canyon, Central Utah, USA Archaic Period, Summer.

Part I

Higher Glyphics

Assembly

a higher assembly
of faraway deities
    sits in admiration
      of their creation and
      all they have made

a higher assembly
      paces pensively, dismayed
      at all the riotous movements

at one time
  it was the best
   but now
    it is only a pile
     of mess they detest
      the scattered remnants
       of rituals lost
       and
         earthly surprises

    slightly below, a congress of birds
   just up there on the wire
  deliberates the changes
in the daily weather

The Standing Stones

let the stones stand at attention
where they are sentinel
                     for moving them
        changes the clock of antiquity
    to a time that only the now knows

        they are the waiters and the
                        watchers
with eyes behind their heads
    and hands that stretch far into
    the depths of then
and off into the infinity of there
way beyond the imagination and
comprehension
  of this place where they now stand
                       protector
guarding a mystery and a folk
of lore and dimension
that we can only see and feel
in the etchings and cicatrices
carved in their basaltic demeanor

let the stones stand as teachers
      zoned into the icons of memory
   and as seekers of the gifts beyond
      the rolling hills where they reside

     stand beside them
and listen to their lithic whispers
and to their secrets that they tell
in lunar rhymes and solar flares
and look where they stare
                and you too
will see where meanings merge

Dolmen Time

tablets of stone spewing out
messages of remembrance
and reverencing ways of thoughts
and beliefs that no longer
insist on the presence of a particular
moment
in a time line

now, they hide a church or mound
of passage from here to there,
or a house with a skew
fragment of stone from a larger
picture of share
a reminder that what is old
is also new

or

tablets of the teachings of *pi;*
a tribute to the role of numbers
ever reminding us of the "eye"
that watches over the pyramid of
time
and to revive us from the slumbers
we are in

so bow down to enter
if you will
if you want to expand the center
of your circle into the infinity of
options
of space and time

dolmen time

time to be still
time to revision

Born Again

it has been another odyssey
along the colossus of roads
that intertwine
through tunnels of love and
misdirection
at times, just missing
the clashing of rocks
that open on to the appealing ways
of acceptance and admiration
yet, at other times, just grasping
all of the *splendors in the grass**
that make up the ever shifting
panorama
of our lives

Scattered Fragments

before the scattered fragments of
now
there was a vast esplanade of
formless infinity
nothing more, just an endless array
of everything

now looking back at then
there's a divulgence of mystery
and mythic implications
that requires years of
ingesting soulful nourishment
before understanding and growth
lest we fear and shrink from
the striking impulses of the
vast unknown

the culture that birthed us
first influenced us
hued us in the colors we came in
then mired us in the isms that guided
us here as we crawled in early
knowledge

then toddled with the urges of
faithless want
and finally venture forth
with a desire to expand

at last we sit and think

way beyond the scattered
fragments of now

Inching Along

We are inching our way along
the murky pathways of our times
through the yards of entangled
choices and overgrown objectives
onto the sidewalks of expedience
where we stop and stare.

A mile ahead to where the steeple
rises
into devotion
and mummified think,

is this the way forward?

Somehow, we seem to always be in
the same spot
even though the landmarks show
the changes
on our way

as we inch along

Journey to the Center of the Core

it·s not so much religion or philosophy
as it is understanding
seeing, perceiving
and unpeeling the skins of illusion
from the fruits of antiquity;
fruits riddled with the sweetness of
myth and divine fabrication

it is more an understating
of stone speak
and cold words
standing over the alignments of
stellar pathways
still left unattended
and mutely tongue tied
into knots of unknowns
that still draw on the lines of antiquity
gone circular around the mystified
moments of now

instead,
it has become a pointed journey
of acknowledgement and
going into the nether realms of
infinity
where one sees
that the true center
of the universe is in the core
of the eye

Chicken Bone Juju

an old chicken thigh bone
sits on a window sill
one end, a boney fist
the other, a penile vulva
arrangement of some sort

the ossified amulet,
excavated from a dig,
speaks of importance
found in a large stone circle
that served as the center
for a fire pit; a seasonal guide
or a place to sit and talk;
sing and dance or simply think

after centuries buried in
decayed rubble and
the ruin of the civilization
that crafted it;
it appeared wizened
stained yet smooth, almost
untouched by time or season

now, it perches by the window
watching wild birds in a feeder
in the tree.

after years of being rubbed between
my oily fingers
sometimes sweaty fingers
or yet at other times
smeared with greasy
potato chip fingers,
it is now a smooth, fine patina
with shiny features

Oh, the companions we
sometimes carry along
are inanimate objects
given a *lifeness* by a touch
a contemplation, moments of
fear or desperation and the joyful*
exhilarations of knowing
that everything is in our hands
be it old or a new found thing
or a decision to make or break
the forks in the road ahead

so much depends
on an old chicken thigh bone

Still Stoned

they etched epics
onto stone books
and erected them
in plain sight
thus spreading their
knowledge across
the landscapes of the future
for posterity

the sketches
many obscure today
display serpents of fire
and chariots of the sun
the alphas and omegas
of a differently scripted era
engraved on horizons that paralleled
different ways
to speak about hypotenuse,
radii, tangent, our universe
and more; much more

but the teachings
remain
a little smudged
by fire, rain and
other rough elements
of climatic change revolutions

the glyphs of knowledge
left on stones
still hold answers to
the questions of the ages
even those we understand not
they still tell tales of the runic
ruminations; of deities and sages
who watched the skies from below
wondering, pondering before
crafting these lithic messages
for us to read, today and ponder
just the same

Small is Beautiful

let,s all conspire to be small again
to breathe together as a unified
body
and take down grandiose schemes
that really are nothing more than
dreams
beyond the winding of the moment
as all things constructed always
seem to melt back into the now

    watch how the tiny ants work
    to build their conical spires of
mud
    constantly on the move being
busy
    yet able to achieve goals that
somehow
    amidst their feverish, scurrying tiny
worlds
    seem to have a path of
knowing

there's power in small
a small tiny frail seedling births a
towering oak
reminding us of diversity in
perception, ideas, ad deeds
insisting we consider all things,
from the simple to the haze
of the complicated, caution**ing**-
that there is looking up and
there is looking down

many hands make light of work
as minutes become hours
and days turn out to be eons
of the far and away
hovering over crumbled palaces
and temples gone drastically astray

pyramids remain in stacks of stone
upon stone
their meanings lost and intention lost
obscured in the passages of time
circles mark the horizons of seasons
still dependent on the comings and
goings of days

grandness is in the eye of aspiration,
in the majesty of spirit
and love in the exultation of simple
corporeal smoke rising from the pyre
off the ground and into the celestial
realms above us;
Ever watchful; constantly building
the towers higher, thus reminding us
that what is really most important is
the warmth in the hearths of our
homes
and the fire in our spirits and minds

let us all conspire to be small again
starting with the little plot in the
gardens
of our souls

People of a Different Mind

      The process of thinking obtusely,
opining differently or
simply regarding dissimilar
perceptions,
involves a subtle shift of view
because seeing is not always
believing.

      Sight can even be deceptive;
refracting reality into prismatic
fragments that crash against our
daily discourses and
strangle strange angles of light;
thus, redirecting a ray into another
version of reality in a different drop of
dimension where down is up
and uptown is downtown
and bad is goodly and good is badly

        This is the way it sometimes
comes to pass,
when strolling in the neighborhood
with people of different minds

Let the Tree Fall

be careful
to let the tree fall
of its own accord
wherever and whenever it chooses

let the tree fall where it may,
of its own free will,
to spread its boughs
and crash into surroundings
that it knows to be a part
of its tribe

let the tree fall when it wants,
regardless of the time
or season
because deep inside its inner rings
it knows
that «where» and «when»
are the prime arboreal reasons
to continue standing; to be tall
and to sing wind songs.

So let the tree fall
where it will

The Geo Logics of Flood

The floods of antiquity continue to
deluge our presence
with unknown knowings about
fractures fission
and intrusions.
It always tends to shove
reasonableness into
another escarpment of elsewhere;
pondering hydrologic turbulence
and aqueous pillorying
that eventually lay down their
ablutions
at the feet of turbulence;

washing into a confluence of erratics
wrongly placed hopes and
projected dreams
that only
got us to this convergence of
disharmony
at the scablands
of severe erosion of the soul
and torment of spirit

to the bluff of now
where loess is more
from hot to cold
real fast and
real furious

we are but glass
fused on to the wheel of time
from the ejected and suspected
etchings of ochre thoughts
onto the walls of the diluvia
diversions of now

this is here

at the rocky convergence
of we

Mending the Fence

Today is mending the fence day
one where we walk along the
barriers of us and them and plug
holes within the system designed
to let in something or keep out
someone we've had a particular
attitude about; both then and now

Here is the opening
where the possum sneaks through
late at night, coming to eat the cat's
food on the patio and foolishly walk
around in a bit of a daze.

Here's where the big black snake
sticks out its head, looking around for
the danger of me with shovel in
hand before slithering into the
garden to find its morsel there to
ensnare and swallow

We let that entrance stay
allowing for an occasional
fool or slimy one-
be that as it may.

And then, there are the creeping
vines, shrubs and bushes; innocent at
first but when left alone
they find an obsession with taking
over, under and all around for that
matter.

Sometimes, they fool you with their
aroma, the beauty or their lilting
curves and siren ways. Truly, some
are all that in the splendor of their
hues
and their bonnets of pinks and
blues and reds

But then, there are those with thorns
that prick you till you bleed and your
blood colors the sister seeds buried
beneath

Then again, there are birds perching
above;. They come, sit, watch and
sing. They come from different climes
and tribes - orioles, doves, jays,
thrushes, crows. They sing their own
songs of joy and love.

They whisper secret bird migration
sounds until their kin stop to join in.
this all breaks up when the hawk,
watching from above, swoops in,
leaving but a pool of bloody wings
fluttering birdless on the ground

These are but some of the
pains of mending your fences

Sitting in a Long Gone Bar
(In remembrance of Tim Buckley's song
Sitting in a Hong Kong Bar)

sitting in the bowels
of a long gone bar
drinking in the vibes of hopped up
      laughter
and gently stirred lethargy
mixed with icy stares
furtive glances.

Ah, wistful embellishments
with beach umbrellas
and postcard scenes of faraway
places

    what'll it be
she asked hauntingly

    a life on the run
my taunting request

        straight up
        no chaser

The Heart of Greenness

When you come upon the rainforest for the first time, you are surprised to see and smell and hear this stalking green edifice with verdant walls of armor

You quickly realize that there is no easy way in; no easy way out.
You are standing at a gate of unyielding earthly infinity; you're about to enter a vital organ of our very existence

It would seem that because of all the inner jungles entangling the soul and life of our presence, a gateway to another option might provide a way to expunge these hindrances in favor of a new allegiance to searching for meaning and acceptance in the present

Even though you stand with fear
the path into the primordial unknown
is irresistible

You enter the cathedral of density
you are there; in it. You are now
behind the green door

Your first reaction is one of sensory
astonishment as you appreciate the
overwhelming realm of another time;
one dominated by acrid smells and
bird cries; searing colors and hues
melting all around you and the
imminent sound and feeling of wet

The early afternoon is raucous quiet,
a foreboding of serenity in which the
oneness of the cacophony is a
harbinger of sudden change.
That's the way of the jungle
in the forest of rain

It rains all the time - a constant
barrage of downpours, of torrents,
of drops, of moisture. It is a hot house
under a damp canopy where
humidity engenders the urges of
fertility and growth magnificence.

Growth reigns from here to eternity-
from the raw to the now; from the
spines of the spineless to the vines
linking the murk to the heavens and
the streams of light that sprinkle
through.

So you have a choice! One of
hesitation and willingness; a choice
between coming and going; or
between activity and passivity.
Whether you stay or go depends on
being aware an awareness that you
are being watched, by a multitude of
eyes,
as well as being the watcher yourself.

Are you a misfit denizen or a well-fit caretaker?
Or perhaps lost on a pathway of adventure and avarice for the riches that do indeed lurk everywhere in the woods - in the muck of the leaves; in the skins; in the steaming mud that sucks at your feet. Everywhere!

In this infernal womb, you are immediately wrapped in a psychedelic awareness that nothing makes any difference here. It is a game of addition and subtraction. You eat sometimes, and other times, you may be eaten

There are moments of slither and moments of flight; those of ever present growl and those of ease; feelings of bite and torment. You howl and dither at the riverside just watching splash along the banks.
Finally, you wonder how you became an extension of this chimera of herbs and chemistry.

The stuff that hangs and the plants that ooze are sometimes the cause of the constant cries of grief and capture.

The swish of tails running away to hide from the claws of evolution;
The smirking of the prey over their recent catch;

These are the other sons and
daughters of another mother-time.
Children of some distant father all
interconnected. The greenways of
another ancestral voice.

This is not urbanity for sure
This is not rural by any stretch
This is the deep forest where night
Falls at the forest door.

This is the heart of it all

Triple Plays

While a wheel can roll with rounded certainty,
the nature of triangles is to hold their ground.

Triangulating the circles of time ways,
leads to a core understanding of intuition that derives itself from a geometry of strength,
perfection and beauty.

Turning into a pointed triadic object that seems to waver and shape shift when prodded in the wrong direction,
is the shimmering reality of a triangular pyramid basking
in a solar embrace.

We understand three sided
Conversations that entangle
Themselves philosophically
Into long stretches of inflected
Night times

We comprehend division of labor
And the partition of time zones into
Circles of standing stone; and
We innately know that three is a
crowd;

But still,

We lack the willful ability to see the
holy spirit nestled deeply in the
retention of our third eye!

Sun Spurts

the sun spurts forth
another flower
on the morning of a full moon
from a seed
planted by a bird farmer;
and cultivated by
a family of earthy nematodes
worming their way
silently,

among the bird songs

Take the Fifty Fifty Road

We're on a journey in search of self
and for a definition of reality.
It is not a pyramid scheme, not at all,
but really just a fifty-fifty chance
a veritable fork stuck in
the roasting road of time

The choices are very simple really
You can say yes or no!
You can go up or down.
You can go in or stay out!
The choice is always yours.

It's a fifty-fifty house of cards
Built on the ruins of another's game
It's a bit charred with eons of fire,
but all the same, a fifty-fifty spin.

The truth remains,
it was a yes or no,
that got you here.
It wasn't a maybe,
that led you here.

This Is Not a Weed

this is not a weed
putting on a pretty
face to confuse you
for a floral minute
while it prepares
boldly,
to invade the
peaceful nature
of your garden
of earthly delights

no!

it is indeed
another member
of the working crew,
waiting for the moment
to get in it and provide
the purpose it was meant for-
to thwart intruders or insects' flights

Gladly so!

this is not a weed
but a part of the larger plan
to cooperate and seed
as only plants in their biotic world
can.

this is not a weed

told you so,

this ain't no weed!

In a Vara Way Land

From an ancient Zoroastrian text:
"Into Vara they brought the seeds of every kind of tree and every kind of fruit...two of every kind to be kept inexhaustible there"

long ago
stored in seeds
under ground
from whence they sprang,
was the future of the subtle,
insignificant grains, wrapped in time.
It became the pollen of a new way

Crossing into an unexpected
otherworld, waiting out a dark acrid
rainstorm on the underside of a
bleeding leaf. It waits, just waiting
for the spring in anticipation of the
ever present surprise of seasonal
regularity and a new array of
forbearers.
It germinates among the fields of
dreams to feed the beastly
awakenings and to give rhyme to
the bee endeavors

It grows with songs of the birds, who
now harbor among the fallen trees
and new branches of a civilization.

It rapidly changes
by starry intrusions
deeply penetrating
the chittering chills
of glaciers gone mad
in the course of an
eternally flaming universe.

Has it dawned on us yet
that there was no beginning
and there is no end in sight?
As we look backward and forward
through an infinite lens
of the divine, we see -

No more water ahead.

It's the fire next time.

Push Has Come to Shove
(a little ditty)

push has come to shove.
the wrong has come to right.
up is down; and under is over.
it's all upside down
when push comes to shove.

push me around,
call me names,
lie to my face;
and play your games

but just don't,
push me aside.
oh just don't,
crush my pride

'cause push has come to shove
the law is in our hands
it's all about this and that
and if you look
you can see the light.

because push has come to shove
the light shines from above
when push has come to shove

About the Author

Jack Kolkmeyer studied English Literature/Creative Writing at Ohio University in the 1960's where he developed a special interest in the Romantic, Imagist and Beat poets. He was the Editor of **Sphere**, the Ohio University literary magazine, from 1967-68. His writings have appeared in numerous publications including **The Writers Place** and **The Liberian Literary Magazine** and have been broadcast on his popular Santa Fe radio programs, **The International House of Wax** and **Brave New World**, and presented with his performance group, **The Word Quartet**. Jack currently reads some of his work on his new radio project, **Fifthwall Radio**.

He was a Peace Corps Volunteer in Liberia, West Africa from 1969-72 and was greatly influenced by the emerging writers of that time, especially Leopold Senghor, Chinua Achebe and Amos Tutuola. Jack received an MPA in Public Policy/Urban and Regional Planning from Indiana University in 1974.

He moved to Santa Fe, New Mexico in 1975 to study filmmaking at The Anthropology Film Center and worked there professionally in education, broadcasting and the performing arts, journalism and urban and regional planning. Jack currently resides and writes in Delray Beach, Florida where his current writing projects include poetry, music and city planning topics, and screenplays.

www.ingramcontent.com/pod-product-compliance
Lightning Source LLC
Chambersburg PA
CBHW061300040426
42444CB00010B/2441